CROCUS BOOKS

RAINBOWS IN THE ICE

Poetry by disabled writers

A collection of new poetry from seventeen talented writers. They range in background from an ex-teacher to a secretary, and from an industrial chemist to a freelance writer. All now live in the North of England, but their roots stretch from Scotland to the Caribbean, from Wales to Wigan!

RAINBOWS IN THE ICE

Poetry by disabled writers

RAINBOWS IN THE ICE

c r o c u s

Acknowledgements
The poems below have been previously published as indicated:

'I cry out', *One Foot on the Mountain* (Only Women Press)
'I am Being Born a Woman', *One Foot on the Mountain* (Only Women Press)
'Friendship', *Disability Arts Magazine*
'Bitter and Twisted', *Disability Arts Magazine*
'Disabling Thoughts', Greater Manchester Coalition of Disabled People Newsletter

First published in 1992 by Crocus

Crocus books are published by
Commonword Ltd,
Cheetwood House,
21 Newton Street,
Manchester M1 1FZ.

Commonword gratefully acknowledges financial assistance from the Association of Greater Manchester Authorities, North West Arts Board and Manchester City Council.

Produced by Wordsmith, Progress Centre, Charlton Place, Manchester M12 6HS.
Printed by Manchester Free Press, Jersey Street, Manchester M4 6FP.

British Library Cataloguing-in-Publication Data.
A catalogue record for this book is available from the British Library.

Contents

Introduction

This exciting collection of poetry explores the full spectrum of human emotions. The seventeen writers featured in this book portray a variety of lifestyles and experiences. They have been brought together in *Rainbows In The Ice* to demonstrate the wealth of creative talent that exists within the disabled community. Anger and wit are used to spotlight oppression in poems such as 'Disabling Thoughts' by Alison Silverwood, 'Check-list' by Keith Stephens, and 'Thoughts of a Cripple' by Sally Convey. More intimate emotions are captured with rich and original imagery in poems such as 'My Dad' by Caroline Ball, and 'Tense in the Taxi' by Aspen.

Disabled people are rarely given the opportunity to speak for themselves or to express their creativity. All too often, we are presented with stereotyped images of disabled people – pictured as powerless victims, deserving not of constitutional rights but charity and pity. *Rainbows In The Ice*, by its very nature, serves to challenge this. It provides a mirror for the thoughts and feelings of many disabled people.

Rainbows In The Ice is a truly entertaining and inspiring book, which expresses a 'cautious optimism' about things to come.

We would like to thank the members of the editing panel for their invaluable support in selecting work for this publication. The editors were Gareth Jones, Ruth Salisbury, Alison Silverwood, and Di Williams.

Cathy Bolton
Commonword

A Cautious Optimism

Chris Murray

Mine is a cautious optimism.
It's usually my mind and not events
That disturb my equilibrium...

Out of the blue it comes
I might be reading
Eating or smoking
It comes down
Flap flap flap
A vulture after my bones
I shun all intercourse
And am at home with nothing
My watch tells me it is two in the afternoon
But I can't wait for the night's release.

Once I imagined women were the answer –
There was a time of tenderness
Lost in a maze of mental turmoil.

Prayer, which some call meditation,
Has proved a worthwhile stand-by
But is it prayer or self-deception?
Let a man dream while he can!

And so I cultivate a cautious optimism.

Tense in the Taxi

Aspen

tense
in the taxi
touching slightly
hold fast
look at each other
smile
look away
pink dawn
rainbows in the ice
numb
disbelieving
reality: you are leaving me
fairytale sky turns
lavender in pain
sadness cuts like
needles into
uncertain daylight.

Shopping

Caroline Ball

I've never been alone in a butcher's or a baker's
  shop,
where your head's below the counter
and you can't catch their eye.

Shopping alone was a long time ago
with a bicycle basket on the side of my chair;
down the tarmac drive and over the dyke,
across the bridge with no sides
where Mum used to worry sky-high,
but Dad would say
'Let her go and see if she comes back'.

Outside the supermarket
butterflies funny in my stomach,
I squeezed the hooter on my chair,
the black hooter to call the man
to read the list in my purse
to bring the goods from the shop shelves,
where I could not go.

Shopping in the basket,
butterflies now flown,
electric as my chair
I whizzed along the quiet lane
home:
to Mum – anxious with barriers of love,

to Dad – loving by letting me go
to grow up,
to try it alone.

Captivity

Valerie Carr

The tiger paced his cage
Frustration, rage
In every taut sinew.
Smouldering hate
Wafted summer-heat
Smell of zoo.

I felt his yearning
For space,
To run, hunt, mate,
In forested freedom
Distanced from ice-cream crowds.

Loosen chains
Break barriers
Escape to wild veldt –
Glorious freedom –
Far from a wheeled chair.

White Horses

Barbara Horrocks

Some December days escape,
shrug off winter's shackles
flirt with spring.
Fingers of sun slice clotted clouds;
wind creams horses' manes from waves.

Sheltering in sand dunes
I watch the sea curl and break,
see endless ranks of stallions
race to freedom;
feel hot flare of breath
smell salt-flecked foam on lips
hear hooves thunder.
I touch knees to flanks
urge my steed towards the Rubicon,
taste jubilation.

Celebrations are brief.
Winter renews its grip,
smothers sunlight,
gelds wild spirits beneath a tea-time moon.

Back home
I hug hands to a mug of tea
toast buns before the fire,
wrap myself in comfort.

Somewhere a stallion whinnies
a white wraith
rearing in the darkness of my mind.

Some December days escape.

The Rain

Aspen

the rain lashing at the side of my face
the wind is whipping thin grass sharp
and the hair from my head
the cold sea is washing
rock bones, the strong sun
swelters my body in sweat
and the full river
crashes mad boulders
downstream
                    the earth is
a tough lover.

I Recall

Chris Murray

I recall roaming rural roads reciting
The poetry of Seamus Heaney –
Now that's going back a bit.
I was in Ireland for the
Kilkenny Arts Festival
With Frank and we were sleeping rough.
It was there we met
The doctor who was a dead ringer
For Solzhenitsyn.
He took us home one night
A mad dash along country lanes
And him over the limit.
After waking one of his sons
So that we might know a decent night's sleep
He explained the bidet to us
And said: 'Be sure to use it now'.
In the morning the sun
Played havoc with our hangovers;
Still we took to the road
With a sense of purpose.
Soon we had a lift with two Americans
Who took us to Waterford
Where Frank's brother lived.
More booze more poetry more life...

Now Frank's in California
And I'm in Manchester

He’s prospering
I’m writing poetry.

I am Being Born a Woman

Aspen

I am being born a woman
I have a soft body
I am made of soil and water
and I look like a tree.
I have quite a few scars
but I am growing more beautiful every day –
not more perfect, just more me.

I have lost quite a lot of blood
at the hands of jagged men
cultivating me for commercial interest,
I have removed myself from their cultivated
plots
where every tree must strive to look the same
and be quiet and obedient
and bear fruit (of the right kind)
at their bidding.
I have picked up my roots and wriggled my
toes
and moved out gingerly into the world.

I have not always had enough moisture to
blossom forth.

The earth sometimes seems filled with storms
and blizzards
long juddering winter, icy immobility,

weary exhausting prostration
squirming, breathless summer.
Yet I see clearly the light on the water
the dazzling patterns, the shimmering leaves
the richness of our different timber
the love in the meadow
the drifting breath
weaving spells of a peaceful spirit.
I feel strength in the blood-rich earth
our tides and threads
mingle
spinning webs of change
the forbidden eating forbidden fruit.

Outside the Forestry Commission we roam the
hills
and sniff life.

In My Head

Jennifer Hoskins

dreams
that are stillborn
don't completely die

but are left
like cobwebs
festooning my opinions

like the acrid
bitter smell of smoke
after a party

someone's thought
colours conversations
I have with my head

Haiku

Val Smith

Haiku on White

Doctors in cold coats,
Closed hospital walls, and ghosts,
white is frightening.

Haiku on Beige

Like my Widnes home,
My own space, my computer
Helping me to write.

Comic

Emma Gleadall

Father, at Christmas
After a drink you were sad,
Aunts and uncles merry,
Mother kitchen busy.

I don't think you liked
Holidays from work and
Part-time writing
'Comic Songs & Patter'.

Sometimes you'd open the case,
Unfold the clown costume,
Sort dried up tubes of grease-paint,
Shake the ginger wig.

After Boxing Day
The stranger left.
You were back to being
my cheerful dad.

Even later in the ward,
A favourite of the nurses:
Still the surreptitious cigarette,
Still coughing blood.

The Shaving Mug

Malcolm G. Cooper

He would rise from the warm water, transformed –
The dusty mendicant that trudged
To the front gate, cast in grimy
Tide-marks about the bath.
The hooter's drone presaged the
Clatter of clogs on paving, and
Seated on the bedroom sill, watching
The smoke billow from the tall
Stacks, hearkened to the familiar
Footfall, that by and by would
Pause and turn into our door.
Gantries moved silently to and fro,
Holding the hoard of twisted scrap
In their hypnotic thrall, whilst
Bombastic locos worried the wagons
About the marshalling yards.

A summons from the bottom of the
Stairs – the house filled with
The aroma of fried bacon.
The bathing ritual done,
They'd had breakfast: and he,
Seated at the fireside warm-clad
In woollen undergarments, bald
Pate polished and pink, would
Recount the events of the night,
Conjuring the fiery glow that inflamed

The heavens, and the cascading
Sparks, as the molten metal decanted
Into the ladle, to the shrill of
The teemer's whistle – shadowy
Figures engulfed in smoke,
Gripping their sweat cloths in
Their mouths, dexterously levering
The heavy covers onto the moulds,
Arms raised in the face of
The ferocious heat.

The table cleared, the shaving
Ceremony could begin, the mirror
In place, and the shaving pot and
Towel brought.
A considered glance at the
Reflection, and a thoughtful prod of
The chin, then final adjustment to
The light, and a careful application
Of badger bristle to shaving stick
Before the white foam was lavishly
Spread to the grey stubble.
Wasn't it time we were ready?
And what of last night's problems:
Were they done?
The head inclined, razor in hand, the
Ceremony would resume, nose pinched
And the upper lip erased of its
Bristle, whilst we busied ourselves
With our satchels, then hurried
Farewells, and we to school, and
He to bed.

There remain a few faded photographs
And the shaving mug, treasured fragments
Of those times. When last I was
There, the sign spoke of ‘Land for
Industrial Development’; the dog’s tail
waving in the willow-herb. And the
Hand that held the cup? Beneath
the grey stone inscribed ‘In Loving Memory’...

For Those Not Yet Angry

Jennifer Hoskins

Okay, I want to set up
a little scenario here,
can you for a moment
just imagine that you

are walking happily along a
path (and, yes, I know walking
is hard for some – but if
it is you'll find this whole

exercise easier) when around a
corner you espy a set
of steps and there are say,
eight of them and as this

dawns (your thinking hasn't been
too good lately) you realize
that you haven't the strength
to climb these steps and instead

you have to turn back or maybe
sit down and rest somewhere
(but there isn't a bench) or maybe
you could go very slowly and

take half an hour over them
and someone will ask you

(sarcastically) if you're waiting
for a bus. Yes, I know you've

been here before and you're
accustomed to seeing giant
obstacles where other people barely
notice concrete steps but this

time before you turn back I want
you to pause and consider
and to become perfectly
clear in your own mind that

you don't deserve this and to
ask yourself how you actually
feel about it and how I
want you to feel is furious.

My Magic Arm

Susan Heatherbell Fletcher

Sometimes it goes up,
Sometimes it goes down,
Sometimes I can't stop it from waving around.
But it is my arm, my magic arm, a part of me.

Sometimes it causes havoc in the dining-room,
Knocking off the table forks and plates and spoons.
I hold it down,
I tie it up,
I put it behind my back,
But it does the things it wants to do,
Not the things I tell it to.

It pulls down curtains and knocks pictures off the wall.
It knocks friends and family, and makes them fall.
But it's still my arm,
I have to live with it, you see,
No matter what it does
It's still a part of me.

The Hulk

Chris Murray

We would not be satisfied
Until we had investigated
The broken wreck
That beckoned us distantly.

A long tramp up Tramore's sands
Brought us close up to the shell
Whose back had been clean-snapped
In some raging, watery inferno.

We climbed her side, peered over and in:
No sailors graced her decks –
She lay violated, deprived of dignity –
Her inners bleached and shone in the August
sun.

We stared long and hard;
Exotic secrets we could only guess at;
The foreign shores she'd nudged
Left no impression on board.

'You'

Aspen

You –
waving your palm fronds
and oozing smells
driving me crazy
with your wet warmth
I paddle my craft
around your shores
still surprised and frustrated
at your greenhouse walls.

I had thought I was welcome
or even invited.

I could've pushed it
you told me later
but I don't like the thought of
sneaking round doors
and I can't stand the sound
of shattering glass.

The Ice

Jennifer Hoskins

Nothing is broken
between us.
Yes, we talked but now
I am silent
and in awe
of your poise
and delicate timing.

This perfect presence
– so rare in men –
reminds me of another
and yet when I scouted
behind your walls
I found more

than insecurity. And wanted
to know you. Now,
you ask after my silence
and when I am honest
you tell me every move
you make is that of

an actor, and you have found
that all you own will not
bring you to trust the
people you meet. And I am
wondering if all I have learnt

can – one day – bring your
trust to me.

You'd Cast Us Off

Keith Stephens

You asked,
Why are we here?
We answered
'We are here
Because you were there',
In Africa
In India
In the West Indies
Et cetera, et cetera, et cetera.

Exploiting, getting rich
from our sweat
Teaching your false religion.

Now, 'cause we are wiser
Now, 'cause we have awaken
From a deep slumber.

Now, 'cause we've said
Enough is enough
'Cause we would rather
Make our own mistakes
Choose our own destiny
You'd cast us off.

Country Churches

Barbara Horrocks

Country churches smell of dust,
damp dim-lit mustiness
and hassocks worn thin
with countless supplications.
Stale incense hangs on the air,
mingles with ascending prayers
traces patterns
on crude crucifixes.

Country churches smell of time,
spilt blood-taint of wine
and beads slipping between fingers
to count ancient litanies
beneath the stained-glass glow.
Penances pricking like thorns, scold
the transgressor
wipe out his sin.

Country churches smell hushed,
with lingering essence of vows shuffling
at the communion rail,
and the tissue-paper touch
of christening robes.
Sometimes they smell cold as coffins
where the muffled tread of bearers
hollowed altar steps.

We thread coins into the collection box
to save the roof; repair the fabric;
preserve the scents of time.

In Memory of Joseph Chipperfield

Chris Murray

The silent sounds of the monastery
Stole over my soul
Imparting a kind of peace.
It was here I met
The aged writer whose body
Was useless down one side.

'What brings a hedonist to a monastery?'
I tentatively explained
About a love gone sour
As milk no cat would look at twice.

'This sacred centre,' he remarked,
'Means more to me than all this dying world.
It was here many years ago
My one true love dwelt.
I had the choice: love or America –
I chose the latter
And so I come here yearly...'

He is dead now, gone for good,
But I still have his books,
Which I fondly handle in moments of reverie,
Hardly aware of the sounds outside my
 window.

Thoughts of a Cripple

Sally Convey

You disablist bastards!
You only do it so you can cope.
My being disabled occupies so
infinitesimally tiny a part of my waking day,
I can exist for days and scarcely think of it.
It is only you who
seemingly can think of nothing else.
What is hard to bear is
the patently obvious fact of your fear,
Your cringing embarrassment that I exist.
I only want to be thought of and addressed as
a fellow human being!
Disability is not a special interest group!
Don't put me in a box, and don't ghettoize me.
Once this momentary fit of anger has passed
I am a reasonable person.
If you feel impelled to help me
Lobby your MP –
and get the gaps removed from the pavement!

Caring

Sheila Leftley

You are not to blame, my love,
so no more conscience pangs, or guilt.
It's on experience such as ours
that the strength of life is built.

Consider this,
that in the midst of joy, of procreation,
a mother stands appalled with realization,
that this tiny perfect scrap,
flesh of her own kind,
is lying there, totally dependent on her care,
is trapping her, no freedom now,
with ties of love, with time she has to share.

How much more, for you, my love,
must these demands and needs of mine,
be problems for you now, be thieves of time.
And all the tears.
Though they're tears of sheer frustration.
And far offset by smiles, my love,
of my appreciation,
of all you do, to make this partnership of ours,
a thing of perfect beauty,
and never use, within this partnership,
the bitter word of duty.

Just Strolling

Malcolm G. Cooper

The locoman, oily rag on regulator,
Leaning from the window, peering ahead.
A glimpse of the late morning light
On tidal waters, seen through a swirl
Of soot and steam; the air laden
With the sweet smell of gorse, and
Bearing the distant bleat of lambs;
The path edging the bulwark
By the lambing pens, and across
The main line to the farmyard,
Where wagging tails belie bared teeth
And ferocious growls: the whitewashed walls
Bright in the uncertain sun, then
Beneath the boughs of the regal
Elm, past the orchard, and round
The bend to halt abruptly: sparkling
Springs polish the pebbles, replenishing
The wayside pond. First on this tuft,
Then on that, now in the hedgerow,
Then mid-path, so to the top of the
Rise and rest at the five-bar gate.
The tall hedgerows focus the brittle
Beams, brightening the celandine that
Gleams on the verdant bank, where
On sultry days coil venomous vipers.
Onwards, climbing the gradual gradient,
The path nestling beneath dancing

Catkins, sheltered by the imploring
Boughs of the crab apple tree that would
Escape the tangled wilderness
Of the abandoned garden – the house
Claimed by the birds nesting in
The ivy garlands draped about the
Chimneys.
Here soon will stand the
Tall foxgloves, their speckled bells
Rivalling the tropical charm of the
Exotic orchid, and in the autumn the
Branches will groan under clusters
Of rounded yellow ripe fruit.
Through the wicket gate and amidst
The flock who chorus their greeting –
The arthritic ewe, hobbling
Painfully and beset by her insistent
Offspring.

Another wicket gate, the territory
Of a chattering magpie, fearful
For her unkempt nest nearby, and
On to the country lane to the brow of
The hill, and the broad vista of
The vale, dominated by the black pall
Slowly drifting o'er the sweep of the estuary:
Traffic, miniaturized by distance, threads its
Way to the golden bays of the peninsula
Beguiling promise of the blue-grey hills.
There the frowning towers of the Norman
Keep, and o'erlooking the elbow,
Where span road and rail, the Roman

Fort, itself companion to
Sentinel spire – the road traversing
The hills forested with the
City's overspill

The hooter's dolorous drone
Reverberates around the
Estuary's empty expanse and they, purposeful
As soldier ants, advancing on
The front gates: time to cut along
Home, and lunch.

At Mrs Whittaker's, Canal Street

Emma Gleadall

Although occasionally house flies
Harbour in the counter display case
Between the machined cream pies, meat pies
The industrial Swiss rolls that face
Teacakes riveted with currants; there
Around eleven, if you call you'll
Get a fried bacon sandwich. It's where
You wait for your cup of tea to cool
Sitting on a sack of potatoes.

Yesterday I saw this woman. Such
A lumpy jumperful, like swedes; nose
Gross as a twisted carrot; not much
Hair, scalp parsnip bare. She was holding
This exquisite cabbage from the net
Of sprout tops. Dark, bossed green enfolding
Frilled emerald. How I did covet
That vegetable treasure, neat leaved
As any cathedral rose-window.

Oh, fresh green flower
Scattered with the drops of crystal,
Cut from wide gardens under
January dawns of amber.
And sometimes a grey pearl sadness.

The Wisteria Blossom

Aspen

The wisteria blossom
dangles temptingly in the garden
though I walk through a wood
of smiling errors
with no right to say
when I will go through a tunnel
or walk naked across the glittering sands.

My cat grips the prey
sometimes loosely
sometimes tight,
the light slides in and out of night,
sometimes I am tasting petals
and
sometimes I am spitting dung
I am losing pieces of the jigsaw
but because of you
I am walking in grace.

Some of my fruits are now ripening at last
as the blinds slip further down
time mocks me
with inspiration
in this bed which is my haven
and also my prison
the spirit is eager
and shakes chains at the devil

my instincts are a battlefield
but there is love here always
you send me dancing through the rainbow
and because of you
I am walking in grace.

Because of you
I am walking in grace.

'A few dried sticks of geranium'

Sally Convey

A few dried sticks of geranium
and the wind whistles through
It is cold in the winter garden.
I see nothing but the complete wreck
of Nature. It is as if the world
were weeping for some
endless inconsolable grief.

The sky is not so inimical
to man it looks brighter
and better today.
What shall I do with this endless
longing and desire I have.

Winter has laid a cold hand over
the garden.

In Praise of Darkness

Chris Murray

I equate darkness with security.
There's no real privacy in daylight –
Just a glaring raw reality.
When I lie in bed at night just before
Dropping off I feel at my most safe.
So that when I pray:
'And let perpetual light shine upon them',
I can't help thinking that when I die
It's darkness I'll be after.

My Dad I

Caroline Ball

Africa means home,
home and Dad;
my big playmate,
strong enough to crack jokes.

Together we adventured in the aga heat,
swimming in swirled waves,
racing the royal blue Chevrolet,
flying the speedboat. Wow!
Water splashing our smiles.

Just me and Dad,
the high-necked giraffes,
the crashing rhinos
and the layabout lions.

I was little,
and safe as a piggyback.

My Dad II

Caroline Ball

I'd trust my dad with everything
except my hair-style or my washing;
difficult for a man alone,
he'd mix the whites with all the colours,
a snowy blouse turned muddled pink.

He cooked his sausages to perfect charcoal,
Saturday's smoke a signal of his need.

Across the road, Marie,
cakes rising miraculous from her oven.

I knew her first,
pretty, with highlights in her hair,
music blaring Englebert.

When he asked if he could marry her,
I said, 'Yes'.
Happy, yet with feelings mixed
like colours in the washer.

She Once Wrote Poetry

Jennifer Hoskins

She once
wrote poetry (when she was
young) and people said
it was good and
she should publish
but she was too shy,

and later wrapped them up,
gave them to her son
for safe keeping.

(Later still, he threw them away
thinking them
not important.)

She says
daughters are best, sons
mean well but they are
less reliable
less practical
less considerate.

She tells me
to publish mine.

Sister

Jennifer Hoskins

I love her so hard that it hurts,
These days it seems everything must
Hurt with a fury extraordinarily obtuse
For such still silent months as
These have been. My little sister
Miles away in shared living quarters
Drinking and laughing
                    perched in her lectures.
I know she'll be dazzling
Them all...

I'm crawling, wounded, howling,
Misled,
Bleeding and blinded

By her light.

Disabling Thoughts

Alison Silverwood

You know it's a funny thing
but the more we try to do for those disabled
people
the more they seem to sneer and shout
and who can understand what they're talking
about?
We promise them everything
and somehow they're never convinced
we really mean the best
and this time
we're really listening.

I dare to want to change.
I get angry
time and again
at the needless strangling
of countless lives.
You like courageous victims, but
who says *you* can tell me
who to be?
I'm not a heroine
and shouldn't have to be.
Sometimes I feel so ill and exhausted
visibility is so hard
I don't like hostility
and I'm not scared of what people think
but yet I am:

thoughts can be dangerous.

We don't know what they want
It's a complex subject
individuals with individual needs
It's all a question of money!
Realistically, there just isn't enough
even for the new by-pass
but especially not
to adapt the buses
Let's try to be practical:
we'll streamline the benefits system
so that less people can qualify,
throw a few crumbs so we can
sweep away all those unpleasant, demanding people,
Get them out of the road
Get them off the screens
Get them out of our hair

Would you mind telling me what this is all about?
If you'll just take your brakes off, madam.
I'm just an ordinary citizen
trying to do my job.

What's an 'ordinary citizen'?
Is it
Patronizing policemen?
Politicians dangling carrots?
Mrs Nice on TV, smiling and challenging,
and saying she really doesn't think

we're speaking for everybody?
We're ordinary citizens
disempowered
because we don't fit
an ideal. You pretend to have no power –
You ask us to be reasonable
while *you* aren't.

Are you afraid of us?
reflecting your own fears –
pricking your own fragile mortality
with nothing visible to replace
that stupid confidence?
too afraid to admit
in spirit we are one?

Listen:
Your weakness is more
dangerous than
my physically challenged strength
because you
are disabled
by your thoughts.

Lost

Aspen

I'm lost
in a sinking feeling
hollow
bereft, all my friends
have gone walking
and I remember what it's like:
everyone going together,
easy companionship
excited adventurers –
memories
crowd my
sensibilities
and leave me
swamped.

I omitted to make plans
and slipped into
emptiness
stumbling
without direction
I have missed my footing
but will not play a losing game
I have a masterly trick
to assuage such pain
and change the view:
comforting music
a nice table-cloth

and a date for one
with a good meal
and a book:
I hope they don't come home
before I do!

Sacrifice

Valerie Carr

Plunging icy depths,
grappling finger-frozen ineptitude.
Abandoned to Arctic quest
of desperate haste to gain a hold
in zero-rated avalanche.
chilled boulders, bruising
crushing aching limbs –
raw, frost-bitten but triumphant,
she waved aloft her trophy
from the freezer waste lands.
He'd wanted lamb for lunch.

Presently it's Christmas

Sheila Leftley

I don't feel disabled
with the family each day.
They understand my diction
and concur with what I say.
The way we talk and rule the world,
share everything, together.
We walk, we ride, we visit, dine,
in laughter, joking, spend our time,
get despondent? Never!
I don't feel disabled
when there's washing-up to do.
Just make a mental comment,
what's a dirty dish or two?
That untidy study has a charm
in its disorder,
that cobweb in the corner
has a preservation order.

But when you're wrapping presents
when Christmas comes around,
when you're knee-deep in tissue
and tags and twine abound.
My fingers twitch, begin to itch,
how they long to stretch out
to fold and tie that bow.
Hands, please curl that ribbon,
wrists, please shake that snow.

Crease that paper corner,
write cards with Christmas cheer.
Words tremble on my tongue
I bite my lip, suppress my fears:
Please catch that end of sellotape
before it disappears.

Butterfly

Barbara Hill

Butterfly
what secrets
you hold.
Against all odds
you spring
into life,
find a mate,
keep the motion,
like a circle,
intact;
From caterpillar
to
chrysalis
Comes hope,
freedom
to evolve
as you spread
wings.

In to be Out

Chris Murray

Some people collect stamps
Others hangovers
while Frank, he collects shrinks.
Has it anything to do with heredity?
His father nursed a bad head
All his adult life
And died a sad old man
After decades of ECT.
Frank has left Ireland
Where mental illness is still taboo
For America
Where it is fashionable to be mad.

And so Frank can now be
Considered where it's at,
Sipping ice-cold beer in California
While his shrink sits taking notes
As his bank balance grows
Fatter
And Frank grows
Thinner
With work and worry.

The Prisoner

Keith Stephens

I'm a prisoner of my imagination
Locked in a cell without bars
I'm shackled by chains of emotions
Left to guard my self.

Can't sleep day or night
My eyes are open,
I can see
I'm a living dead
A zombie.

Voices are all around me
Bidding me to go free
Break out, they say
No walls surround you
You're a prisoner
Of your imagination.

I look around my cell
The bars I see are made of steel
The chains I cannot break
My brain's playing tricks on me again.

What Boredom Can Do

Chris Murray

Like a man with the DTs
I wanted to smash all before me,
Spare nothing, not even the picture
Of the Sacred Heart that smiled

Benignly down upon me.
I was restless, had no money
To souse my sorrows,
Didn't know what to do with myself.

And then I saw my animated
Reflection in the mirror, knew just
What to do to kill a minute or two,
Grabbed the scissors and made for the bathroom.

And in no time at all, the part
That had so reassured me
Was gone, and all I could see
Was a clumsy lower lip looking lost.

Children not Admitted

Emma Gleadall

My son never knew my father;
By a strange quirk of life
He now plays at the Nab Top Farm;

Swings on the same five-bar gate
Where I balanced years ago
Waving my striped school scarf.

After Salford cobbles
Green spaces a tram ride away
I liked the country; missed my dad.

I could see the valley sanatorium,
Long huts, doors opened to iced air,
Patients in overcoats, mufflers, gloves.

I think the distant figure
Who waved a newspaper reply
Was my father.

Soon the special bus would come,
I'd rejoin my mother,
Sunday visit finished.

The sanatorium has gone now.
When I was telling my son
He asked 'What's TB?'

Hidden Courage

Betty Riach

We all have hidden courage
But it takes a cruel blow,
A turn of fate that hurls us down
And leaves us empty, low,
Before we find our inner worth,
Before we understand
That the iron fist of circumstance
Can be a helping hand.

The Breakfast

Malcolm G. Cooper

A thin wisp would escape the chimney,
And I, whistling the dog to heel,
Would climb the hill to the tiny cottage.
'Is it you then?' the stub pinched between
Thumb and forefinger, and flicked in the fire.

'Any luck?' the watchful eyes following
The heavy bag onto the peg.
'That's a nice dinner!' the bloody hare
Displayed at length, held high by the hind legs.

'Where did you get him?' Lifting his cap
And scratching as prelude to the telling.

'You'll take breakfast...?
Remember, it's plain it is!'
The bacon fat spat and the fire flared,
The pan balanced precariously on the piled coals.
'Just a minute!' sandalled feet,
He'd flop round the kitchen, fork in hand,
To flip the rashers, edging the copper kettle to
the flames.
The tortoiseshell cat stretched and yawned.
Then jumped off the fireside chair,
To lap milk left in the saucer
At the foot of the stairs.
'Bring a chair – the one behind the door.'

From the kitchen table, where seated,
He sliced the doorsteps.
'Go ahead you...don't wait,'
Pointing to the plate, knife in hand.
'It's plain it is, mind!'
The bread broken, dipped in delicious fat and relished.

He poured the tea, the handle held in the hairy fist,
The brawny arm reaching across to fill the cup.
'Had enough...? Sure now...?
You've only to say...plain it is, mind you,
Not like when she was alive:
She could cook. We had the garden then.
Runner beans!' Extending the forearm,
Finger on the biceps, indicating length.
'And potatoes!' making a fist.
'Aye indeed!' making to rise.
'Oh dear. The knees,' pulling a face.
'Not so good.'

Replete, we repaired to the fire,
The cat already curled on the rug.
'No, no! A low chair is no good for me.'
He sat propped against the dresser,
Smoking a cigarette, smoke curling about the oak beams.
'Going then? Why not stay a bit?
He's ready for the off!' seeing the dog stir.
'Tell her I'll be down Saturday,' getting to his feet.

'Yes indeed!' eyes twinkling.
'A call at the "surgery" first.'
The door closed. A pause at the corner
To view the estuary, then, dog at heel,
Down hill and home.

Fighting

Sue Norris

We,
us cancer patients,
never envious
nor mad as hell,

fight on
despite others'

prejudices;

and I will be
bad tempered;

and I will be
loving;

and I will be jealous;

putting up with pain,
and you lot
are not doing it;
a lonely business.

Now and again
I will
say,
'Go, fuck yourself.'

I’ve seen people dying,
had enough.

Where were you?

Not with me.
Not with us.

In Patient Without Patience

Colin Knowles

Sombre, pastelled, oxygenated walls
Clicking heels down hollow halls.
Glossy, dour, antiseptic floor,
'No smoking' signs upon the door.

Restless nights of alien sounds,
A TV room that's out of bounds.
Prodding and probing by mechanical hands
The indignation of bottles and pans.

Crisp, white aprons, wearing conditioned smiles.
Bathrooms and toilets made of six-inch tiles.
You arise at six thirty, whether awake or not.
The rest of the day is spent watching the clock.

Visiting times seem to come and go.
Strained conversations of unnatural flow.
Leaving lockers adorned with fruit and cards
Streams of condolences stretching for yards.

Check-list

Keith Stephens

One head
check
Two eyes
check
One mouth, one nose
check
Two arms, two legs
check
Ten fingers, ten toes
check
One standard size you know what
check
Blood red
check
Feel pain when hurt
check
Skin black
check
All attributes of a human being
check
Black *homo sapiens*
check

Outposts

Barbara Hill

How deep
Rich dwelling place
Of the mind,
Out of reach
I search
Hidden corners
To find answers,
Like space
The outposts of my thoughts
Appear,
Just out of bound
Never to be grasped,
Floating like bubbles
Only to be burst
At touch.

Letter to a Neurologist

Sally Convey

Dear Doctor,
After all this I can say I'm happy.
Everything works except my legs –
and my voice is a bit off.
I have revelled in my life,
enjoying it as if for the first time ever.
Christmases at home, Easters, Whits, and those
more private festivals by which we mark our
  lives
I am more than happy to have seen.
Joy is nearer the mark,
joy and delight in the world restored to me
  beyond hope,
for which I daily rejoice,
not forgetting that curious and
terrifying dream from whence
I escaped which will haunt me forever.
Good luck to your future patients, and
I hope their relatives will dare to
put their heads into the lion's mouth
and argue the toss for life.

‘I cry out’

Aspen

I cry out
All you hear is a moan on the wind
I lay forth my truths
you hear a squeak in the corner
I scuttle along and metamorphose
you see bizarre shapes with no meaning
I insist you pay attention
you say my bullshitting is done very well.

I beat you about with my anger
you laugh at my attempts to hurt you
I cover you sloppily in love
you walk away looking out of the corner of
    your eye
I weep in frustration
you catch my tears and sell them to the tourists
I whisper in despair
you pour sympathy on my fallen crest.

I collapse in a heap on the floor
you cart me off to your nearest bin
I create amazing art
you pity my disturbed mind
I sing the most lovely woman-songs
you moralize over my sexuality
I make the most amazing sense
you say you do not understand.

When did you stop listening to me?
Do I have to use words that don't hurt your ears
so much?

Portrait of a Friend

Chris Murray

Should I stand aside and watch my friend
Turn wrecker and wrecked,
A spoiled and spoiling child
Slave to an insatiable ego?

'Renegade priest' he calls himself
As he blazes a sodden trail
Through all the servile pubs
Outdoing both Behan and Thomas.

For the booze releases the furious furies
That shriek along the charred nerve endings
Setting off booby traps of indiscretion
Until insult is the order of the day.

Witness his mouth: eating, drinking,
Smoking, cursing, blabbing, repeating
Himself incessantly, friend only
To the merchants of bravado.

He squanders flattery like five pound notes;
Steeling myself as though threatened by
    needles
I stare groundwards, shedding the skins
Of embarrassment one by one.

Yes, I must stand aside and abandon,

Or else become entangled in the same net,
And spend my days and nights writhing endlessly,
Towards the only end: a pickled brain, a halted heart.

Bitter and Twisted

Aspen

bitter?
yes, i am bitter
like acid, and
like poison fruit.
twisted?
yes, i am twisted,
like an old tree trunk
wracked and gnarled
like old roots
twisting deep in the soil
i am here and i
will not be moved:
i am far too strong
and deadly.

We are Black

Keith Stephens

The fact is we are black
Don't want to change that
Say it again
Don't want to change that
Give us our due
We ask for nothing more
No ladder to the top
No helping hand
Put no obstacle in our way
We'll build our own bridge
Across the chasm of time
We'll fashion our own destiny
Let us build our tomorrows
Remember we have had yesterdays
Experience will be our teacher
Each fumbling footstep
The foundation of our tomorrow

Our Friendship is Mellowed to a Whisper, Sister

Aspen

Living so far apart
your deterioration not visible
I relied on you to tell me
what was going on for you.
You told me nothing:
you said your disability was
a small part of who you are.
I couldn't work out
what was going on.
You didn't help me
I had to guess.
I felt like I was
losing you.

When I deteriorated myself
I felt that I couldn't talk about it
you might think
that was giving in to it,
or making it too important.

What's happened to our closeness?
That valuable, precious
love-gift?
It has trickled away, like
water in the desert, we no longer know

who we are.

Being political about disability
has given me teeth
to eat it.

Deciduous/Evergreen

Aspen

it's true
my health is deciduous
my love,
but feeling
my love is evergreen.

Biographies

Aspen

I am a member of Lesbianspirit Writers' Group.

> the essential spirit
> is a seed within my heart
> forcing unrepentant renewal
> making possible
> bewitching songs.

Caroline Ball

I was born with cerebral palsy and have never been able to walk, or read and write in the usual way.

I spent my childhood in Africa, which I loved, and on our return to England I continued to live at home with my parents for as long as they could manage. Then I came to Daresbury Hall, a residential home run by the Spastics Society. My mum died a while after I moved to Daresbury, and eventually my dad remarried. I am fond of his second wife, Marie; she is like a mum. However, they now live in Crete so I only see them once a year when I stay with them on holiday.

In September 1991, I moved into a purpose-built bungalow in Widnes, which I share with two friends. It is wonderful to have our own front door, and the privacy of my own bedroom. I am lucky to be able to talk clearly and enjoy painting pictures with words. I work with another writer who puts my thoughts onto paper, then we move them around, like making a jigsaw. I began writing less than two years ago, but it is now very important to me. I have so many stories to tell.

Valerie Carr

I was born in Southport in 1935. Due to a fall in early childhood I contracted a 'diseased hip' which was never satisfactorily diagnosed. I spent five years in hospital and did not begin formal schooling until I was nearly eight years old. A further twelve months in hospital at the age of ten lost me more schooling but despite this I attained five 'O' levels. While attending a secretarial college after leaving school I was again admitted to hospital and on my eighteenth birthday was presented with the decision whether or not to have my left leg amputated. I decided to do so, was fitted with an artificial leg, and subsequently went to work in a bank. I took my Institute of Bankers' examinations, passing in Part I and then got married.

With my son and daughter grown-up and independent, I am now pursuing a lifelong interest in writing – mainly poetry – and have had several poems published, and read on the radio. I am presently engaged in researching the life of my grandfather.

Sally Convey

I was born in Wakefield and grew up in Leeds. After grammar school I went on to study at Oxford (Lady Margaret Hall), Newcastle and Leeds universities. Before I fell ill I spent eight years as an English teacher in the Greater Manchester area. I have two daughters, both grown-up, and live in Chorlton with my second husband.

In late 1983, just as the new school year was beginning, I was struck down by a virus. I rapidly fell into a coma and for five months lived in a strange and confused world. My neurologist had long since pronounced me a vegetable when, during a ward round, I waved to him with the only hand I could then use. I went on to spend nearly five years in hospital, fighting to regain control of my body, but have now had nearly four years living in my own home again.

My love of poetry and my determination to write have helped me to get through these years. Almost my first words when I regained my speech were the opening lines of Marvell's 'The Garden'. Although, even with my word processor, I find writing physically difficult, I try to spend part of each day recording my thoughts and reactions to what, in my first (unpublished) collection of poems, I call *The World Outside My Window.*

Malcolm G. Cooper

I am from South Wales, born in Gorseinon, Welsh speaking, and reared in Bynea, on the Loughor estuary.

I was educated at Ysgol Cwmyreag Dewi Sant Llanelli, and Queen Elizabeth Grammar School, Carmarthen.

I graduated at the Economic Honours School,

at Swansea University: obtaining a BA honours degree. I then worked for two years in the steel industry at the Spencer Works, Newport, Monmouthshire. Deciding this was not for me, I became a research assistant in October 1967 to study 'The rationalisation of the cotton industry', at Manchester University where I was awarded an MA in 1969.

I became senior lecturer in applied economics at Salford College of Technology, but regrettably developed Parkinson's disease at the early age of thirty-two years.

I live in Sale, Cheshire with my wife Ann, and son Tomos, aged sixteen years. I started writing for my own pleasure, and have written a number of poems, and am finishing a large work of descriptive stories about 'The day in a life of a steel worker in the 1950s'.

Susan Heatherbell Fletcher

I was born on November 8th 1960 in Queen's Park Hospital, Blackburn. I grew up in Oswaldtwistle near Accrington in Lancashire. From the age of five, I wrote poems with my mother, which were published in a book in 1982. Before the age of ten I was writing stories, dictated to my mother, borrowing TV characters and putting them in my own situations for fun.

For five years I have been a member of the creative writing group at Daresbury Hall. My cerebral palsy means that my right arm has a life of its own. With my left hand I work on a word processor. I paint, using crayons and water-colour, pencil and ink. My favourite subjects are horses, boats and flowers.

I am on the editorial board of the quarterly regional magazine *Disabled Not Daft*, and am now writing a crime novel.

Emma Gleadall

In my early days I joined Robin Skelton's WEA poetry group and his Manchester Peterloo group for contemporary artists. I write poems, short stories, radio and theatre scripts and have won several first prizes and awards.

My stage work has been produced at theatre festivals, and choral verse used in education work. I have worked with folk groups, and now mainly work with retirement and disabled groups. I have been a creative writing tutor for the LEA, WEA and residential colleges, and acted as an editor and adjudicator.

I like children and animals; some people. I have a deaf-blind granddaughter and help in a small way (if invited to give a reading) the charity SENSE which helps the young deaf-blind. I am a steering group member for the local branch of the National Coalition of Disabled People.

After a spot of GBH I underwent a series of hip operations. I have glaucoma. I joined the WAAF during the war and worked in the Ministry of Education on demob. I enjoy life given half a chance.

Barbara Hill

I am fifty-seven years old, married to Dennis for thirty-five years, with two grown-up children – a son, Clive, and a daughter, Jacqueline.

Over the years I have gained many interests, i.e. anything involving crafts, hand and machine knitting, sewing for the home, water-colour painting and playing the organ when I can make the time. Also my poetry which helps the mind to put thoughts and feelings into words to share with others.

I began writing verse in 1981 when my husband bought a CB radio and I began to write rhymes about the callers. I then started making up verse about items in the store cupboard, sending them to the manufacturers with interested responses.

Later I joined a class organized by our local council, Kirklees, where I learnt the art of non-rhyming verse which I enjoy most.

It wasn't until 1988 that things changed for me, from being able to dash around to suddenly finding that I no longer could, having developed poly-arteritis (inflammation of blood vessels) and being classified disabled. I then was introduced to the Day Centre for disabled people in my home town, Dewsbury, where I learned painting and joined another poetry group where we read, write and discuss poetry, and also enter the occasional competition.

Barbara Horrocks
I was brought up in Liverpool during the war and although I lived in Australia for a while, I have spent most of my life on Merseyside.

At one time I was a keen fell walker, and 'Country Churches' was inspired by a tiny church in my beloved Lake District. However, mobility problems – caused by a spinal disease – forced me to give up this activity and to take early retirement from my job as a school secretary. I started writing and have since had short stories, poems and articles published in magazines and newspapers. I have also had three poetry collections published and am currently working towards a fourth. I am a regular contributor to BBC Radio Merseyside, and have had work broadcast on BBC Radio Four's 'Morning Story' slot.

I have three children, all married, and now live with my husband in Freshfield, Merseyside, overlooking the pine woods and within a stone's throw of the red squirrel reserve.

I belong to Southport Writers' Circle and am a member of the Society of Women Writers and Journalists.

Jennifer Hoskins
Born in 1967, I wrote my first poem in a chemistry laboratory some sixteen years later. There on the page was the manifestation of a conflict I'd struggled with for years, I could never decide which was the better way of describing the world,

art or science. Which was more real – the chemical equations or the poetry scribbled in the margin?

Told I was bad at English, I squashed my desire to be a writer and began three happy years at college studying computing, astronomy and pure mathematics. I enjoyed my subjects but couldn't help noticing that poetry was still growing through the gaps between equations and on the waste land that is the back of computer print-outs.

In the summer of 1989 my career development came to a shuddering shaking halt along with the rest of my life. I became disabled. No longer able to walk or read or write, I was emotionally devastated.

I have since been slowly recovering and discovered my major problem isn't my disabilities but the way society responds to (and ignores) disabled people. I have added the disability civil rights movement to my already extensive list of causes and my major ambition now is to change the world. Oh, and to be a writer.

Colin Knowles

I was born in Wigan in 1945 and educated at Wigan Boys' Grammar School and Salford Technical College. I followed a career in textiles and in so doing, I worked and lived extensively throughout the United Kingdom. Then, following a period in East Africa, I emigrated to South Africa in 1980. Having attained my personal ambitions, my world crashed some six years later, due to the onset of ill health. After prolonged hospitalization and my inability to continue my career, I returned, together with my new bride, stepdaughter and baby son, to my Wigan roots.

I recall that I began writing poetry as far back as 1962, progressing to writing and producing local village shows. The pen, however has never been more ready than when asked to write and produce the Ladysmith Centenary Show – a nostalgic collection of drama, poetry, song and prose. This was my finest hour.

Being disabled has evoked many forms of emotive turbulence which I try to pour out as the written word. My first anthology, *Pieces of My Mind*, was in aid of the Wigan and Leigh CT scanner appeal. My second, *Brushstrokes of Painted Words*, is due for publication early in 1992 and will be in aid of another local charity, The John Tierman Cancer Trust.

Sheila Leftley

Sheila Leftley was born in West Yorkshire in 1938 and was educated at St Joseph's College, Bradford. After leaving school she worked as an industrial chemist for eleven years, and then changed careers to become a teacher of chemistry and physics in Lancashire. After teaching for eleven years, acquiring a degree in education and reaching head of department, Sheila was forced to retire in 1983 suffering from motor neurone disease. It was then that she had the time to follow a lifelong interest in creative writing, and began writing poetry and prose. Most of her compositions were written with the aid of a specially adapted word processor, as the disease affected the use of her hands and her speech. Many of Sheila's articles have been published in the Motor Neurone Disease Association Journal, and in the book *Never 'eard of it,* an anthology of work written by MND sufferers and carers about the disease.

In recent years Sheila has been the editor of *Hot Gossip* a magazine published by and for people at the Jubilee Centre in Bolton. In addition she has been assistant editor of *Pulse*, the Ladywell Hospital Magazine.

Sheila's poems evoke the pain and frustration of living with a severely debilitating disease, yet also clearly illustrate her joy of life, and the pleasure she derived from having those she cared about around her. Sadly Sheila died as a result of her illness on December 15th 1991.

Chris Murray

I was born in Manchester in 1949. Brought up in All Saints and attended St Ignatius secondary school. Worked for a year in the now defunct John Heywood's of Deansgate before joining the army. Four years in the Royal Engineers; three years in Germany and a spell of jungle warfare training in South America. Upon leaving the army, I went into further education, gaining five 'O' levels and one 'A' level in English Literature. It was while I was in my first term at Alsager College doing a BA in creative writing that I had my first breakdown. I was diagnosed as schizophrenic. I was twenty-eight at the time and had another breakdown when I was thirty-two. On both occasions I was nursed back to comparative health in Withington Psychiatric Hospital.

My interest in writing was rekindled when I joined a creative writing workshop under the tutelage of Jim Burns, the Preston-born poet. The main outlet for my poetry is *Purple Patch*, the Midlands-based magazine, edited by Geoff Stevens.

Among my favourite authors are Henry Miller, Bernard Malamud and Tennessee Williams. However, my big hero is the musician Van Morrison. I also admire the work of Seamus Heaney and Ted Hughes. In a bid to offset my gloomy temperament, I have recently gotten into the positive thinking books of Norman Vincent Peale.

Nowadays I live in Burnage with my parents.

Sue Norris

I am forty-three, single, and have had an amazing life so far – including much violence, conflict and tragedy. I have a passion for living, although the modern world often fills me with frustration and fear.

I am self-taught. At school I was largely ignored by my teachers except when I was 'difficult'. I have physical handicaps so one school 'highlight' was a star for drying my back.

Over the years I have had a series of close attachments, and have a special friend whom I use as an interface between my needs and longings and the practical necessities of life. Unfortunately, the stresses on my life, have taken me at times to the fringe of schizophrenia.

The space which other people fill with logical structures, I fill with image and feeling. For the last ten years I have poured these into poetry, ranging from rage and grief to images of more delicate emotions.

Betty Riach

I am a senior citizen and have been a widow for over thirty years. I was born and spent my early years in Dumfrieshire but now I am told I speak with a Yorkshire accent. I was introduced to poetry at a class at the local day centre about twelve months ago. I had never done any writing previously but was goaded into making an effort. I now receive great pleasure from my writing.

Alison Silverwood

I am the North West columnist for *Disability Arts Magazine* and a freelance writer.

Val Smith

I was born in 1956 in Ashford, Kent. I had a normal childhood till the age of four, when I contracted meningitis. I remember regaining consciousness and finding myself unable to talk. From then on I had cerebral palsy, needing daily care. I was in hospital for four years. I have a twin sister who is able-bodied.

I had a good education at Kier Park School in Kent, and at sixteen came to live at Daresbury Hall. At Daresbury I study art, and at Halton College I study drama, computer studies and basic home-care.

I have been a member of Daresbury creative writing group for two years, and am on the editorial board of the quarterly regional magazine *Disabled Not Daft*. I am now engaged in writing my autobiography.

Keith Stephens

I was born in Jamaica in the West Indies. I came to England in 1962. In 1974 I became mobility impaired as a result of having meningitis. At the present time I am employed as a local government officer, previous to this I was a radio and television service engineer.

I am involved, a little, with the disabled peoples' movement, i.e. fighting for social justice – the right for all disabled people to make decisions for themselves and thus to have control over their own lives.

My partner and I have got two children. I have got a degree in social science and I like watching most sports. When the spirit move me I will read some non-fiction.

About Commonword

Commonword is a not-for-profit community publishing co-operative, producing books by writers in the north west, and supporting and developing their work. In this way Commonword brings new writing to a wide audience.

Over a period of fifteen years Commonword has published poetry, short stories and other forms of creative writing. *Rainbows In The Ice* is the twelfth title to be published under the Crocus imprint.

In general, Commonword seeks to encourage the creative writing and publishing of the diverse groups in society who have lacked, or been excluded from, the means of expression through the written word. Working-class writers, black writers, women, disabled people, and lesbians and gay men all too often fall into this category.

To give writers the opportunity to develop their work in an informal setting, Commonword offers a variety of writers' workshops, such as Womanswrite, the Monday Night Group, and Northern Gay Writers, and future plans include a workshop for disabled writers.

Cultureword, which is a part of Commonword, and which acts as a focus for Asian and Afro-Caribbean writers, organises the Identity writers' workshop. Cultureword also co-ordinates Identity magazine, and a writing competition for black writers.

In addition to writers' workshops and publishing, Commonword offers a manuscript reading service to give constructive criticism, and can give information and advice to writers about facilities in their immediate locality.

Commonword is supported by: the Association of Greater Manchester Authorities, North West Arts Board and Manchester Education Committee.

The Commonword/Cultureword offices are at Cheetwood House, 21 Newton Street, Manchester M1 1FZ. Our phone number is (061) 236 2773. We would like to hear from you.

Recent Crocus titles

Flame

A dual language book of poetry in English and Urdu by Asian writers. Love, home life, racism and other political issues are some of the areas explored by the fifteen talented poets in *Flame.* Translations are by Alishan Zaidi.

'One of the best collections of Asian poetry I have read.' (Kam Kaur, Eastern Eye)

ISBN 0 946745 85 4

Price £4.50 Pbk

Herzone

Fantasy short stories by women. Ranging from science fiction, to 'twist in the tale' stories and mythical fantasies, this collection has something to delight and entertain everyone.

'There is nothing but pleasure to be gained from these tales.' (Manchester Evening News)

'A varied and satisfying collection.' (Zoë Fairbairns, Everywoman)

ISBN 0 946745 80 3

Price £4.50 Pbk

Beyond Paradise

An original collection of poetry that celebrates the vitality of gay and lesbian writing. Provocative, funny and touching, *Beyond Paradise* offers fresh perspectives on life in the '90s - and beyond!

'I promise you, once you've read it, you'll keep

coming back for another little glimpse of life in the lesbian and gay lane.' (Scene Out)
'The tragic nature of human existence, the fun and joy of being alive are here...' (Gay Times)
ISBN 0 946745 75 7
Price £4.50 Pbk

Relative to Me...
Short stories on family life. Families can be a source of inspiration - or desperation! The stories in *Relative to Me...* show both, with a wonderful mix of serious and light-hearted writing.
'Relative to Me... proves there's plenty of talent just waiting to burst forth from the region.' (Manchester Metro News)
'Twenty refreshingly original tales.' (The Teacher)
ISBN 0 946745 70 6
Price £3.95 Pbk

No Earthly Reason?
Poetry about green issues - *'This beautiful book is a collection of reflections from the heart.' (Toyah Willcox)*
ISBN 0 946745 65 X
Price £3.50 Pbk

Talkers Through Dream Doors
Fourteen talented Black women write about their lives in this collection of poetry and short stories.
ISBN 0 946745 60 9
Price £3.50 Pbk

Now Then
Poetry and short stories illustrating lifestyles, work and leisure from 1945 to the present day.
ISBN 0 946745 55 2
Price £3.50 Pbk

Holding Out
Women's lives are portrayed with realism, frankness and fun in this excellent collection of twenty-one short stories.
ISBN 0 946745 30 7
Price £3.50 Pbk

Other titles from Commonword

Black and Priceless, poetry and short stories.
0 946745 45 5, £3.50
Between Mondays, poetry from the Monday Night Group.
0 946745 35 8, £2.50
Identity Magazine, poetry and articles by Asian and Afro-Caribbean writers. £0.95
Liberation Soldier, poetry by Joe Smythe.
0 946745 25 0, £2.50
Poetic Licence, poetry from Greater Manchester.
0 946745 40 4, £2.50
Turning Points, a Northern Gay Writers collection.
0 946745 20 X, £2.95

For a recent catalogue of all our titles, write to:
Crocus books/Commonword
Cheetwood House
21 Newton Street
Manchester M1 1FZ.

If you are visually impaired and would like this or any of our other titles to be produced on audio-tape please contact us.

ORDER FORM

TITLE	QUANTITY	PRICE	AMOUNT
Rainbows In The Ice		£4.50	
Herzone		£4.50	
Flame		£4.50	
Beyond Paradise		£4.50	
Relative to Me...		£3.95	
No Earthly Reason?		£3.50	
Talkers Through Dream Doors		£3.50	
Now Then		£3.50	
Black and Priceless		£3.50	
Holding Out		£3.50	
Identity Magazine		£0.95	
Poetic Licence		£2.50	
Between Mondays		£2.50	
Liberation Soldier		£2.50	
Turning Points		£2.95	
	TOTAL	______________________	

Please send a cheque or postal order, made payable to Commonword Ltd, covering the purchase price plus 35p per book postage and packing.

NAME..

ADDRESS..

....

.... POSTCODE ....

Please return to: Commonword, Cheetwood House, 21 Newton Street, Manchester M1 1FZ.